discovermore

Life in a Community

Community Workers

Dwayne Hicks

Britannica
Educational Publishing
IN ASSOCIATION WITH
THE ROSEN PUBLISHING GROUP

Published in 2024 by Britannica Educational Publishing (a trademark of Encyclopædia Britannica, Inc.) in association with
The Rosen Publishing Group, Inc.
2544 Clinton Street, Buffalo, NY 14224

Distributed exclusively by Rosen Publishing.
To see additional Britannica Educational Publishing titles, go to rosenpublishing.com.

Editor: Kathleen Klatte
Book Design: Leslie Taylor

Photo Credits: Cover Drazen Zigic/Shutterstock.com; (series background) Dai Yim/Shutterstock.com; p. 5 (top) Caiaimage/Robert Daly/iStockphoto.com, (bottom) Евгений Хабаров/iStockphoto.com; p. 6 Monkey Business Images/iStockphoto.com; p. 7 monkeybusinessimages/iStockphoto.com; p. 8 Carrastock/Shutterstock.com; p. 9 adventtr/iStockphoto.com; p. 10 New Africa/Shutterstock.com; p. 11 flukesamed/iStockphoto.com; p. 13 (top) scarletsails/iStockphoto.com, (bottom) David Tran Photo/Shutterstock.com; p. 14 x-reflexnaja/iStockphoto.com; p. 15 Shinyfamily/iStockphoto.com; p. 16 ake1150sb / iStockphoto.com; p. 17 shironosov/iStockphoto.com; p. 18 shironosov/iStockphoto.com; p. 19 AzmanJaka/iStockphoto.com; p. 20 vm/iStockphoto.com; p. 21 Chalabala/iStockphoto.com; p. 23 (top) Teka77/iStockphoto.com, (bottom) SDI Productions/iStockphoto.com; p. 24 Orhan Cam/Shutterstock.com; p. 25 Bumble Dee/Shutterstock.com; p. 26 FilippoBacci/iStockphoto.com; p. 27 DenisTangneyJr/iStockphoto.com; p. 28 Africa Studio/Shutterstock.com, p. 29 kali9/iStockphoto.com.

Library of Congress Cataloging-in-Publication Data

Names: Hicks, Dwayne.
Title: Community workers / Dwayne Hicks.
Description: New York : Britannica Educational Publishing, in Association with Rosen Educational Services. 2024. | Series: Discover more: life in a community | Includes glossary and index.
Identifiers: ISBN 9781642828788 (library bound) | ISBN 9781642828771 (pbk) | ISBN 9781642828795 (ebook)
Subjects: LCSH: Community life--Juvenile literature. | Human services personnel--Juvenile literature. | Civil service--Juvenile literature. | Communities--Juvenile literature.
Classification: LCC HM761.H53 2024 | DDC 307–dc23

Manufactured in the United States of America

CPSIA Compliance Information: Batch #CSBRIT24. For further information contact Rosen Publishing at 1-800-237-9932.

Contents

At Work in Your Community

A group of people who live in the same place and share the same resources or interests is called a community. In a community of people who live in the same area, there are workers who help all the members of the community conduct daily life. The workers have different jobs and responsibilities that keep a place and its people healthy, clean, and safe. Community workers can include doctors, firefighters, police officers, teachers, and government leaders.

Each community has different needs and resources. A large, wealthy city may be able to afford more workers than a small town can. A rural community has different needs than an urban one.

Teachers, doctors, and delivery people are common in most communities.

compare and contrast

What kind of workers are important in a community that experiences harsh winters? What about one where it's always hot?

Workers trained to remove snow and ice from roads are important in cold weather communities.

Working to Keep People Healthy

Doctors are important to every community. They are educated and trained to prevent illnesses and to heal the sick or wounded. When treating patients, doctors work with many other people, including nurses and therapists.

There are many parts to a doctor's job. Doctors first need to identify what has made their patient sick or where the pain is. Then they decide on a treatment.

This team of doctors and nurses are trained to help people with medical emergencies.

This nurse is trained to take care of small children.

Like doctors, nurses are professionals who take care of people's health. Most nurses work along with doctors in hospitals, clinics, or offices. Some nurses give support and aid to doctors during surgery. Some care mainly for children or the elderly. Others care for patients with mental illnesses. Aides and orderlies assist nurses with their work.

Consider This

Why do you think there are so many different kinds of doctors and nurses? Why do they work in such different places?

Helping People Smile

A dentist is a doctor trained in treating teeth and gums. People go to a general dentist to get their teeth cleaned. It is important to have clean teeth to prevent cavities and tooth decay. Dentists clean each tooth with special tools. If they find a cavity, they fill it in so the tooth stays healthy. Dentists take X-rays to find problems inside the teeth or below the gums. They also treat jaw problems and gum disease.

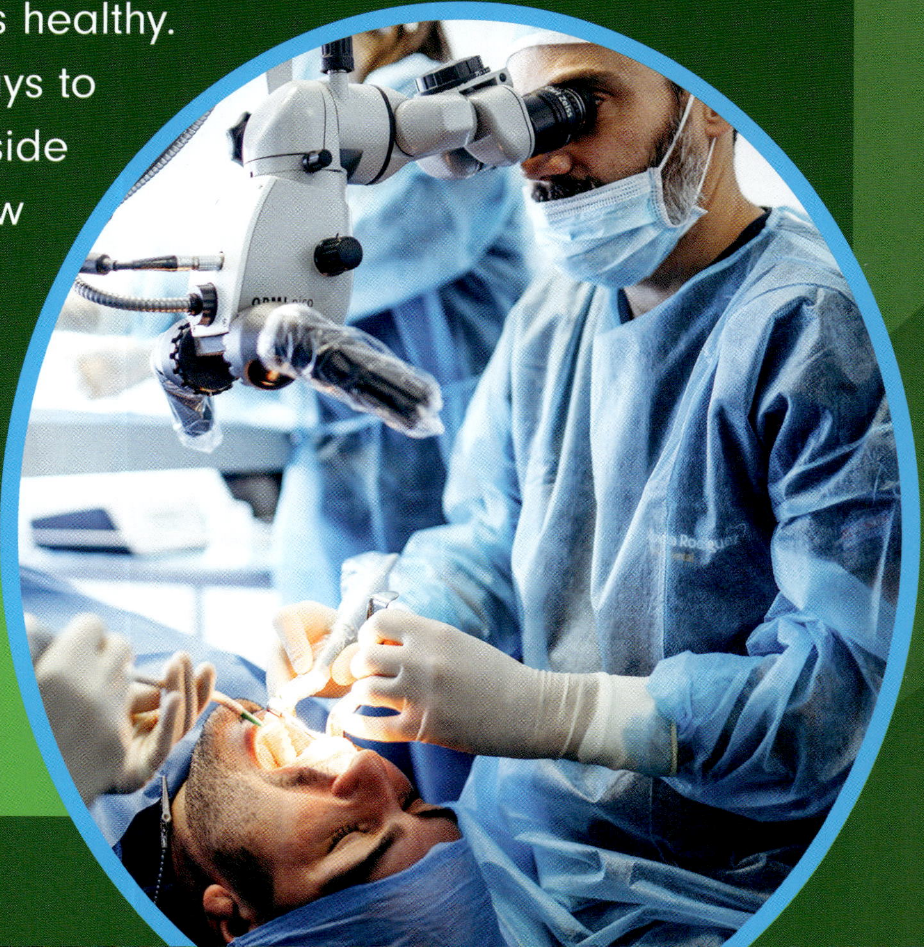

An oral **surgeon** performs surgery on a person's mouth.

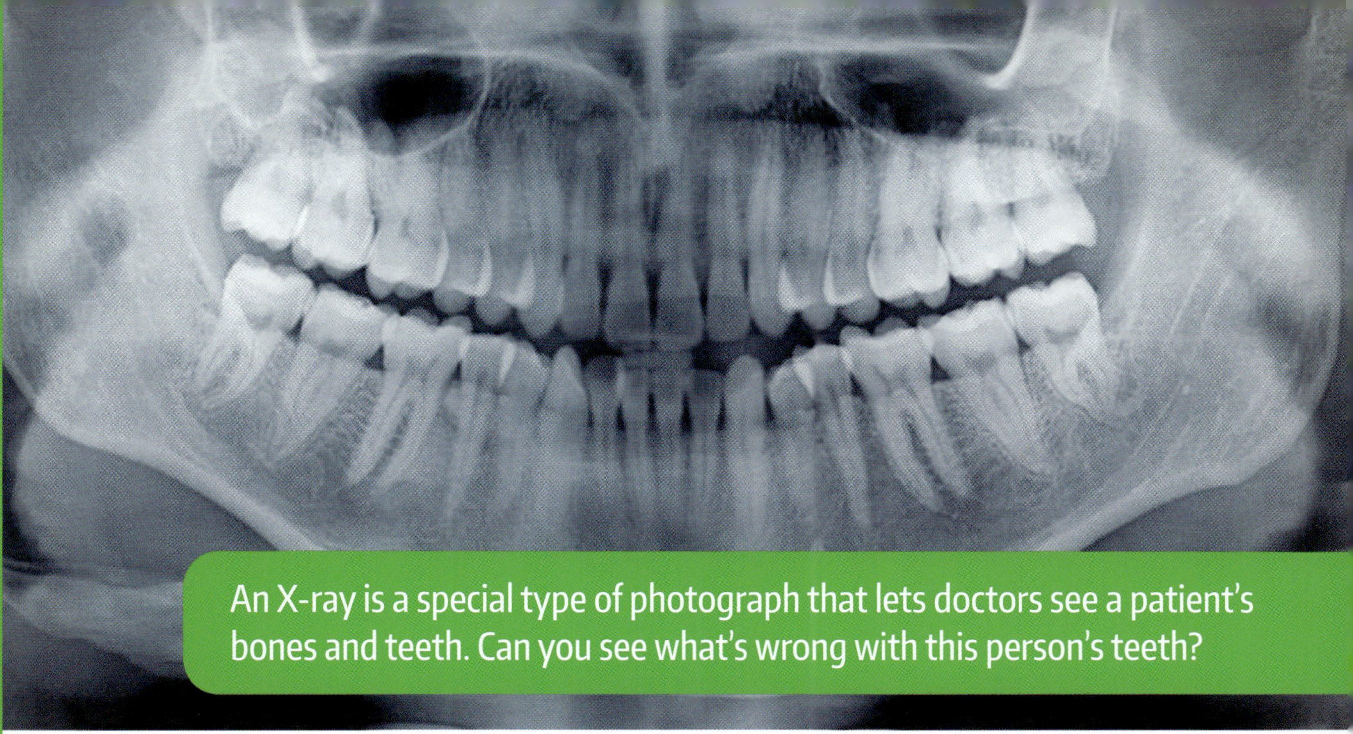

An X-ray is a special type of photograph that lets doctors see a patient's bones and teeth. Can you see what's wrong with this person's teeth?

Many dentists who work in communities are general dentists. They can begin practicing as soon as they graduate from dental school. A small number of dentists become specialists. This means they must go through extra education after dental school. There are nine dental specialties. You may have heard older kids talk about visiting the orthodontist. That's a special kind of dentist who straightens teeth.

WORD WISE

A surgeon is a doctor who repairs a person's body by cutting into it to remove or repair damaged or diseased tissue.

Taking Care of Our Animal Friends

Doctors who take care of animals are called veterinarians or vets. They prevent, diagnose, and treat diseases in animals. They can perform surgery and prescribe drugs, and they also help animals give birth. This branch of medicine is called veterinary medicine. People go to school to become veterinarians. They earn a degree called a Doctor of Veterinary Medicine. Many veterinarians work in hospitals or clinics. Others start their own business, or practice.

Most communities have a vet who treats dogs and cats. If you have a reptile or bird, you may need to look in a larger community for a practice that handles exotic animals.

Sometimes large zoo animals are taught simple behaviors, like opening their mouth on command, to make it easier for a vet to take care of them.

Veterinarians can specialize in different areas. For example, some only take care of pets. Others help in communities with zoos and farms. This is especially important because many endangered animals live in zoos and are in danger of disappearing forever. Farms depend on having healthy livestock to sell and breed.

Consider This

Some vets volunteer their services for special events in the community. They might take part in low-cost spay and neuter clinics (to "fix" pets so they can't have more babies) or free vaccination clinics. How do you think these services help make the community safer and healthier?

Protecting the Community

Police officers are people who are specially trained to keep our communities safe. They work for the governments of towns, cities, counties, states, and countries. The police have many tasks. They patrol, or keep watch over, streets and neighborhoods. They do that by car, foot, horseback, motorcycle, or bicycle. Police also go to the scenes of crimes and emergencies to catch criminals and to help victims and survivors. Some police investigate, or study, crimes to find out who committed them.

Some police wear uniforms. Others work in everyday clothing. Many police officers carry handcuffs, a notebook, and a two-way radio. Some also carry a handgun, but they can use a stun gun or pepper spray to stop criminals without seriously harming them. Police officers attend training academies to learn about the law and how to handle their weapons and equipment.

Some police officers work with dogs. The dogs might be trained to sniff out explosives or drugs.

compare and contrast

Some police officers protect our country's borders. Others protect a single small town. Which do you think is more important? Why?

Transportation Security Administration (TSA) agents are a type of federal police. They help keep people safe when they travel.

Keeping People Safe

Firefighters are often referred to as the Community's Bravest. They're specially trained to put out fires. Some firefighters also investigate the cause of a fire. Teams of firefighters work quickly to keep fires from spreading. In cities, they connect hoses to fire hydrants for water. In small towns or out in the countryside, there are no hydrants. In these areas, firefighters use tanker trucks to bring water to the scene. In addition to putting out fires, firefighters may need to rescue people trapped inside burning buildings. Firefighters also respond to nonfire emergencies, such as road accidents and medical emergencies.

Firefighters check their equipment each time it's used. They need to know that everything is ready to go when an alarm goes off.

Firefighters try to prevent fire from happening. They do this by checking to see that buildings have clearly marked exits, working alarms, and fire extinguishers.

Some firefighter positions require medical training. For these positions, firefighters need to be certified as emergency medical technicians. In many small towns, firefighters are volunteers. That means they are not paid. Whether they're professional or volunteer, all firefighters are trained to do their jobs safely. They learn to handle their equipment and work in teams.

Consider This

Why is it important for public buildings to have smoke detectors and fire alarms?

Educating the Community

Teachers are one of a community's most valuable resources. The main job of teachers is to encourage learning. They help students learn new things about the world and the people in it by explaining important facts and ideas. They also guide students in finding information and thinking about ways to solve problems. Teachers may work in a school building or they may lead classes online.

During the COVID-19 pandemic, many kids went to school via computer.

University professors hold advanced degrees called doctorates. They might also travel to do research and publish papers about the topic they teach.

Teachers usually teach students in particular age ranges. In the United States the main ranges are: elementary (ages five to ten or eleven), middle (eleven to thirteen or fourteen), secondary (fourteen to eighteen), and college and **university** (adults). Teachers of young children teach all subjects. As students get older, teachers tend to specialize in specific subjects. Some teachers go on to become school administrators. They might be in charge of a single school or all the schools in a community.

WORD WISE

A university is an advanced school that grants degrees in the arts and sciences.

Building a Community

A community always needs to have new buildings constructed, or old ones repaired. The people who do this work are called construction workers. They perform heavy physical labor and often work outdoors in all types of weather conditions.

Some construction workers have particular skills. Concrete workers pour concrete foundations, glaziers deal with glass windows, and ironworkers install iron and steel beams and columns. Electricians, plumbers, and carpenters all work on different parts of a building.

This construction worker has headphones to protect his hearing when he operates loud machinery.

Construction workers build using plans drawn by **architects**.

Other construction workers have more general duties. They are known as construction laborers or helpers. Sometimes workers use bulldozers, trucks, and diggers (also called backhoes) to move dirt to prepare construction sites and to make roads. They may operate cranes to load and unload building materials.

Safety is always important at construction sites because many of the jobs are dangerous. Workers wear safety glasses to keep dirt and debris out of the eyes. Hard hats protect heads from falling objects. Construction workers often wear bright, neon-colored vests to make them more visible.

WORD WISE

An architect is a person who designs buildings. The printed plans construction workers use are called blueprints.

Keeping the Community Moving

Transportation workers are the people who move people and goods around your community. They may transport raw materials, such as food, minerals, and wood, to factories where the materials are made into products. Other workers then use trucks, railroads, or ships to move the products, such as clothes, shoes, and furniture, from factories to stores.

A dockworker is using a crane to load cargo containers onto a freight ship.

A helicopter pilot might report on traffic conditions, airlift accident victims to hospitals, or carry tourists on sightseeing flights.

People in some communities also rely on transportation workers to get them to their jobs or to school. Bus and streetcar drivers and **subway** and train operators provide public transportation throughout big cities. School bus drivers safely deliver students to school. Other transportation workers in communities regularly collect and haul away garbage and recyclables in trucks. Airplane pilots help move people and cargo quickly between different communities.

WORD WISE

A subway is a system of underground trains.

Making Deliveries

Mail and packages move through communities using postal services. People mail their letters and packages by placing them in a mailbox or taking them directly to the post office. Postal workers sort the mail according to its destination (the place where it is going). They may sort it by hand or with the help of machines. Postal workers tie sorted mail in bundles and put it into sturdy sacks. These sacks are marked with the mail's destination.

Postal workers send the mail to its destination by truck, train, ship, or airplane. Postal services around the world cooperate so that mail can even travel between countries. There are also private delivery companies people use.

Private delivery companies often cost more than the post office, but they promise faster delivery.

compare and contrast

Some mail is delivered in one or two days, or even overnight. How do you think that happens? What kind of workers are involved?

At a post office, workers help people send mail and packages. They also help them adjust their delivery if they're going to be away from home. People can even buy shipping supplies and cool postage stamps.

Governing Large Communities

The United States is a large community made up of many smaller communities. The national government (also called the federal government) oversees the whole country. Leaders in the federal government do many things. They defend the country from outside enemies, keep order within the country, and provide services for its people.

The federal government passes laws that apply to everyone in the entire country. For example, the legal voting age in the United States is eighteen. No state or local government can tell someone older than eighteen that they can't vote.

It's better for some decisions to be made at the state level. Hurricane-proof houses are a good idea in some communities. Others might need snowplows and salt. Still others might need equipment to fight forest fires.

The federal system has three separate branches that work together. Elected leaders in the legislative branch make laws. An elected president is the head of the executive branch, which carries out laws. The judicial branch interprets laws through courts.

Each state also has its own government. State governments are organized much like the federal government. The people of each state elect a governor and other leaders to run the state. Each state has a court system as well. State governments are responsible for maintaining things like bridges and roads in their state. They also provide things like emergency services, based on the needs of their state.

Consider This

Why is it important for some laws to affect the entire country, but not others?

Governing Small Communities

Smaller communities also need a government. A city government usually includes a group of elected lawmakers called the city council. In some cities, the people also elect a leader called a mayor. In other cities, the city council names a leader called a city manager.

Being mayor of a large city like New York or Los Angeles is a full-time job.

In a small town, the mayor might hold a regular job. They might be someone people run into at the store or at church.

The powers of a mayor or city manager are determined by the law. Some mayors are so powerful that they may actually run the city. They **enforce** laws, manage public services, and oversee city budgets and projects. In other cases a mayor leads the city council but cannot act on his or her own. Sometimes mayors act mainly as a symbol of the city, while the city council holds most of the power.

The leaders of city governments manage many community services. They're responsible for things like emergency services, education, maintaining streets, and trash collection.

WORD WISE

To enforce a law is to make sure people obey it.

Volunteers in Your Community

People who work to help others in their community without being paid are called volunteers. Volunteers may help families who have lost their homes, clothing, food, and other things after a flood, hurricane, or earthquake. Some people volunteer to protect animals or the environment, or to coach sports teams.

A volunteer at an animal shelter helps cats become accustomed to people. This makes it easier for them to be adopted.

A volunteer reads to kids at the local public library.

Young people can volunteer in their communities in many ways. They might pick up trash in their neighborhood or in a park. They might also collect canned food for a local food bank. Volunteering can involve walking a dog, raking leaves, or shoveling snow for a neighbor who is elderly or ill. Volunteers often plant and water flowers or vegetables or pull weeds at a school, neighborhood, or community garden. Schools often need volunteers to help run booths at events. How do volunteers make your community better?

Consider This

In some communities, volunteers deliver meals to sick or elderly people. Why is this important?

Glossary

carpenter: A worker who builds or repairs wooden structures.

city council: Elected officials who work with the mayor to set laws and run the community.

city manager: A person hired by the city council to run a city.

diagnose: To recognize (a disease, illness, etc.) by examining someone.

emergency: A situation that calls for immediate action that would otherwise result in a large amount of harm or loss.

government: A group of people that makes laws and runs a community.

ironworker: A worker who makes heavy iron or steel products.

mayor: An elected official who acts as a head of a city or town.

medicine: The science that deals with the prevention, cure, or easing of disease.

patient: A person under medical care and treatment.

plumber: A worker who puts in or repairs the pipes and fixtures that support the distribution and disposal of water.

rural: Of or relating to the country, country people or life, or agriculture.

survivor: A person who stays alive after an emergency has ended.

therapist: A person trained in methods of treatment other than the use of drugs or surgery.

treatment: An attempt at healing someone who is sick or wounded.

urban: Of or relating to the city, or a thing that is from the city.

For More Information

Books

Moening, Kate. *Cashiers*. Fairfax, VA: Bellwether Media, 2020.

Moening, Kate. *Delivery Drivers*. Fairfax, VA: Bellwether Media, 2020.

Moening, Kate. *EMTs*. Fairfax, VA: Bellwether Media, 2020.

Websites

Family Volunteer Day

www.pointsoflight.org/family-volunteer-day

Points of Light offers a guide to volunteer activities families can participate in together.

Meet the Helpers

ny.pbslearningmedia.org/collection/meet-the-helpers

PBS Learning Media has a series of videos about helpers in the community.

Index